TRUE
SEA
ADVENTURES

TRUE
SEA
ADVENTURES

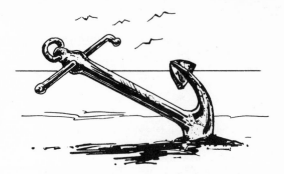

Donald J. Sobol

THOMAS NELSON INC., PUBLISHERS
Nashville   •   New York

First edition

Library of Congress Cataloging in Publication Data

Sobol, Donald J
    True sea adventures.

    CONTENTS: In the belly of a whale.—Horror ship.—The unsinkable Captain Boyton. [etc.]
    1. Seafaring life—Juvenile literature. 2. Adventure and adventurers—Juvenile literature. [1. Seafaring life. 2. Adventure and adventurers] I. Title.
G525.S595   910'.45   75–20425
ISBN 0–8407–6454–5

FOR

MY NEPHEWS

PETER AND SCOTT

CONTENTS

TRUE
SEA
ADVENTURES

FOREWORD

The strangest sea story of all occurred when some primitive man first pushed a log from shore and rode across a patch of water. Since that dateless event, the sea has witnessed the unending drama of men and ships.

Many of the best sea stories, I am certain, have never been put on paper. They exist as hearsay, as the folklore of seaside towns, or as fragments in mariners' museums. They excite the ear and eye, but to track down details is a hopeless task.

From the welter of true stories that have survived the passing centuries, I have selected twenty-two. They fascinated me when I first read them. They fascinate me now. With the pleasure of sharing a pleasure, I have retold them for boys and girls.

All twenty-two accounts belong to a bygone day—to a time when the air was pure, the water clean, and men took to the sea still believing that a boat could carry them to paradise.

D. J. S.

In the Belly of a Whale

In February, 1891, the whaling ship *Star of the East* was cruising off the Falkland Islands in the South Atlantic when her lookout shouted, "There she blows!"

Ahead rose the spout of a giant sperm whale. Instantly the ship put on more sail and gave chase. Within half an hour, her crew could make out seabirds standing on the great mammal's back. Two rowboats were lowered.

The last man into the second boat was James Bartley, twenty-one. He took an oar and, all unknowing, began to pull toward one of the most astounding dramas of the sea.

Ahead of him, the first boat had reached within striking range. The harpooner stood. His muscular right arm whipped around, hurtling the new bomb lance—a harpoon with an explosive charge—into the leviathan.

The whale rolled and twisted in the agonies of death. Sixty feet of monster, weighing a ton a foot, thrashed the water into heaving mountains of foam.

An upward lash of the mighty tail caught the second boat. The twenty-five-foot craft was tossed into the air like a matchstick. The men spilled out, stunned and helpless. But the whale had done its worst. Mortally wounded, it was quickly killed.

The crew of the first boat rowed over to rescue their comrades in the water. All were accounted for save two. One man had been seen to drown. The other, James Bartley, had simply disappeared.

Aboard the *Star of the East,* Captain Wedderman noted the missing men in his log. After both names he wrote, "Drowned." There was no other way to explain the loss of James Bartley.

Too much work lay at hand to allow time for mourning. The dead whale was hauled to the ship and lashed alongside. Swiftly the crew fell to removing the blubber.

At midnight the work stopped. The weary men went below to catch a few hours of sleep.

At dawn they were up and back at the task. The huge stomach was hoisted onto the deck.

Suddenly a seaman yelled. He pointed to the stomach—to a spot that moved with the slow, steady rhythm of breathing.

Captain Wedderman was summoned. Carefully he made a cut in the tissue. A shoe appeared, and then a leg. Inside was the missing sailor, James Bartley!

The digestive juices of the whale had bleached his hands and face to a pasty white, and he was doubled up and unconscious. But he was alive!

His shipmates quickly freed him from the ghastly dungeon and laid him on the deck. A bucket of icy seawater brought him around. With a scream of terror he struggled to his feet, tottered to the railing, and collapsed.

He was carried to the captain's cabin. There he lay for two weeks, strapped to the bunk, a raving lunatic. By the third week he showed signs of recovering. After a month he was well enough to insist upon taking up his duties aboard ship.

Of his horrible experience, he recalled only the opening seconds.

He remembered being hurled out of the rowboat and then sliding into darkness. His hands met a slimy surface that shrank from his touch. Breathing was not difficult, but the heat and odor were overpowering. He passed out and knew nothing until he opened his eyes in the captain's cabin.

That he lived was a miracle which can be explained, perhaps, by two facts. First, he was lodged in the part of the stomach nearest the throat, and thus he continued to receive air. Second, the whale met its death right after swallowing him and so cooled off almost at once.

The voyage was James Bartley's first aboard the *Star of the East*—and his last.

When the ship docked in England, the modern Jonah made straight for his native city of Gloucester. There, until his death eighteen years later, he worked as a cobbler.

Horror Ship

Hoodoo, jinx, curse . . .

These are some of the names given to the invisible forces of evil that cannot be explained, but which bring terror and even death from out of the unknown.

The Russian freighter *Ivan Vassilli* was preyed upon by such a force. It crouched in the ship's corridors, prowled her decks, and crept into her rigging.

The *Thing*, as it became known, may have been merely a fantasy dreamed up by frightened, superstitious seamen. But what it did was real, horribly real.

Its victim, the *Ivan Vassilli*, was built in 1897 and for five years traveled the trade routes untroubled and unnoticed. Then, in the autumn of 1903, she was sent with a cargo of military supplies to Vladivostok. En route, the *Thing*, somewhere and somehow, got on board.

As the steamer neared Port Arthur, a sailor, Alec Govinski, suddenly began to scream. His screams and his scrambling unnerved the rest of the crew. Panic arose and spread out of control.

For twenty minutes men raced about the ship, seeking blindly to escape they knew not what. They were men under a spell—until the crazed Govinski threw himself into the sea. Abruptly the panic passed. It was as if the death had satisfied the *Thing*, for the time being.

Men lay panting on the deck, exhausted, dazed. The spell of horror had lifted. But three days later it came again. Some of the seamen insisted they beheld a misty form gliding toward them. That afternoon the steamer reached Vladivostok.

Several of the crew deserted. They were captured and turned to unloading the cargo. The captain and first officer stood over them with pistols.

Her hold emptied, the *Ivan Vassilli* put out for Hong Kong ahead of the winter ice. The trip was a nightmare, the ship a prison of horror. Two seamen committed suicide. One died of fright. Three days before docking at Hong

Kong, the captain, Sven Andrist, jumped overboard.

No earthly power could make the men stay on the *Ivan Vassilli* now. When she tied up at Hong Kong, the entire crew deserted with the exception of four men: two Swedish sailors, a Welshman named Harry Nelson, and Christ Hanson, the second officer.

Hanson was given command as reward for his loyalty. Filling out his crew with Chinese and lascars (East Indian sailors), he took on cargo and sailed for Sydney, Australia. The day land was sighted, the *Thing* struck again. Hanson shot himself.

At Sydney the *Ivan Vassilli* lost her second crew. The fear-stricken men jumped ashore and ran off as fast as their legs could carry them. Only one man, Harry Nelson, had the courage to remain.

A new captain was sent to Sydney. By withholding mention of the *Thing*—which in private he ridiculed—he signed on a fresh crew. After four months of hauling cargo around the Pacific, it seemed the *Ivan Vassilli* had shed her horror. The captain openly scoffed at Harry Nelson's tales. He set course for America.

The *Thing* had only been waiting. After the steamer passed Honolulu, it struck three days in a row. Three men leaped into the ocean. On the fourth day, the captain shot himself. In San Francisco a seaman hanged himself. In Boston another swore that invisible hands had pushed him from the rigging onto the deck.

Harry Nelson alone stayed with the ship and eventually helped bring her back to Vladivostok. Try as he might, he never solved the mystery of the *Thing,* except that the men recovered their reason as soon as it had claimed a victim. Once a man died, it seemed temporarily content and withdrew.

The *Ivan Vassilli* lay in the harbor of Vladivostok, her engines idle, her decks deserted. No amount of extra wages could bribe seamen into serving on her. As the years passed, she became an increasing nuisance and finally a menace to shipping. She was towed away and burned.

The Unsinkable Captain Boyton

To the list of forgotten heroes of the sea add the name Captain Paul Boyton.

He called himself "captain" though he never skippered a ship. He didn't need one. He gained fame and fortune paddling thousands of miles on his back!

Boyton was born in Dublin, Ireland, of American parents, in 1848. He was raised in Pittsburgh, Pennsylvania. As a boy, his favorite pastime was swimming in the Allegheny River.

With the years he grew into a handsome daredevil of a man, restless for adventure. He served in three wars, shipped as a deckhand, and hunted diamonds in South Africa. Swimming, however, remained his first love.

The summer of 1873 found him in Atlantic City, New Jersey, heading the first lifesaving unit at the blossoming resort town. He personally saved, or claimed he saved, seventy-two bathers from drowning.

Whatever the true number, he came to the attention of C. S. Merriman, a rubber manufacturer. Boyton had youth, courage, and the silver tongue of the born salesman. Merriman had an invention, a rubber suit that held air. The two men teamed up. Together they hoped to sell the suit to swimmers, thereby saving lives and making themselves rich.

Boyton's job was to demonstrate the sensational new lifesaving device. He paddled miles out to sea in tests off the Jersey coast. But his real work began at nine o'clock on the night of October 21, 1874, aboard the ocean liner *Queen* as she neared the Irish coast.

Over his regular street clothes he donned the rubber suit and inflated its air pockets. Then, gripping a paddle and a waterproof bag of food and water, he waddled to the ship's railing.

"Good night, captain! Good night, ladies and gentlemen!" he called out cheerfully.

The enthralled passengers watched him go over the side and plunge into the Atlantic Ocean. Fifteen miles away was his destination —Cape Clear, Ireland.

Unfortunately or fortunately, a gale came

up. More than fifty craft were lost that night in the storm. Boyton, now buried by the raging waves, now popping up like a cork, made it to land. He became a hero overnight.

Invitations to lecture at healthy fees poured in. A natural showman, he was soon giving polished performances all over Great Britain. After each talk he withdrew briefly from the stage. He reappeared in front of a screen painted with the black cliffs of Ireland, wearing his rubber suit and holding up his double-bladed paddle and an American flag.

An exhibition before Queen Victoria encouraged him to try paddling across the English Channel. He started from Dover, England, on April 10, 1875. With a boatload of newspapermen nearby, he made his way toward Boulogne, France. Strong tides kept him from his goal, and he had to be picked out of the water.

The setback did not hurt his name one pennyworth. Telegrams of congratulations on a splendid effort arrived from people of importance in England, including the queen and the prince of Wales. Boyton overcame the disappointment of the Channel failure by lecturing at $250 an engagement.

The following month he attempted the Channel again. This time he started from Cap

Gris-Nez, France, with a few improvements. He put on his two-piece rubber suit, which weighed thirty-five pounds and covered him everywhere but the face, and entered the water at dawn on May 28.

At a quarter to eight he called to the small boat following him for the first of his improvements—a tiny sail. This he fixed to a little mast in a socket attached to his foot. Later he requested a cigar and a bugle.

Puffing and tooting, paddling and sailing, he reached Dover in twenty-three hours. He strode ashore waving a tiny flag. England lionized him.

So did the rest of Europe once it got a look. He gave exhibitions wherever there was water, paddling feet first at the rate of one hundred strokes a minute and firing off rockets.

Gradually he enlarged his program till it offered such attractions as building a raft from wreckage, sending messages by carrier pigeons, cooking, shooting, fishing, and rescue work. As a climax, he destroyed an "enemy" ship by torpedo.

Triumph followed triumph. He staged a mixture of an aquatic and Wild West show that ran for two seasons in London. In America, his exhibitions earned him nearly $2,000 a week.

His success as a paddler far outdid his success as a peddler of rubber suits, however. His fame is a matter of record; royalty decorated him with a chestful of medals, cigars were named after him, and songs were composed in his honor. But sales of the inflatable rubber suit are unknown. It is doubtful if he ever sold one.

In his prime he paddled down most of the rivers of America and Europe, and the money rolled in. When age finally forced him to retire, he continued to travel widely and in comfort.

It was while returning from a trip to the Caribbean in 1924 that he caught pneumonia and died at the age of seventy-seven.

The Last Torpedo

Before she killed herself during World War II, the United States submarine *Tang* had already won a place in naval history.

In less than twelve months in the Pacific, she sank thousands of tons of Japanese freighters, tankers, and transports. Her officers and men had a proud boast: she seldom wasted a torpedo.

Even without a target in her periscope, the *Tang* had proved a heroine. During an air strike against the island of Truk, she played the role of lifeguard, and her rescue of twenty-two downed American airmen remained a record for more than a year.

Yet all her earlier feats paled beside her fifth patrol, from September 27 to October 24, 1944.

Her skipper, Commander Richard H. O'Kane, had wrung permission to go it as a lone wolf. The *Tang* set off boldly for the Formosa Channel, which no American sub had penetrated.

The risk was great because the Channel was heavily mined. However, enemy captains tended to relax, thinking themselves safe. O'Kane hoped for a parade of targets. He was not disappointed.

On October 6, the *Tang* weathered a hurricane and four days later slipped through a minefield between Formosa and Sakashina Gunto. The morning of October 11 she sank a small freighter and she got another that night.

"We were clicking," Commander O'Kane remembered.

Entering midchannel, the *Tang* found nothing. She made for the China coast to try for a task force reportedly moving north. On the way, a light cruiser and two destroyers eluded her by swift zigzagging. So off she went to Turnabout Island by Haitan.

Not long after midnight of October 23–24, her periscope picked up a convoy bound for the Philippines. Bearing down on her were four freighters loaded with planes, a transport with more planes, a destroyer, and a few small escort vessels.

Torpedoes were shot from bow and stern, wrapping three freighters in flames. The fourth freighter and the transport pointed for the *Tang*, intending to ram her. She slipped between them, and the Japanese ships collided!

The destroyer opened fire. "It looked like a good place to get away from, so we cleared the area at full power," O'Kane recalled.

For a few hours the *Tang* took a breather in deep water to the north. Then, before dawn on October 24, she returned to Turnabout.

No targets appeared all day. But after nightfall, the sub's radar showed a solid line of pips across the screen. The *Tang* started tracking the biggest convoy any of her crew had ever seen.

Near the coast of Fukien, the *Tang* went to work. She sank a triple-decker transport right off. Stern torpedoes accounted for another transport and a tanker at ranges of six and seven hundred yards.

It was a submariner's dream until the escort began firing salvos. "Things were anything but peaceful now," remembered O'Kane. The *Tang* broke off.

She put five miles between her and the Japanese destroyers before slowing down. Two torpedoes remained of the twenty-four with which she'd started the patrol. Although she

structure and put up the light. The placing and fitting of every timber, rod, and stone he had overseen personally. He had put into the tower his brains, his sweat, and his time. It was his masterpiece. Although unusual, he was certain it was the safest place on earth.

The light worked well for several years. In 1703 it showed signs of needing repairs. Winstanley waited for a long series of young gales to pass before starting for the lighthouse reef.

On Thursday, November 25, there came a lull. At dawn on Friday, Winstanley sailed with his workmen from Plymouth. They arrived at the lighthouse in good time.

Late that day, quicksilver in barometers began dropping alarmingly. The skies darkened and then unleashed a furious monster of a storm. By 1:30 A.M. the wind had reached terrifying strength and raged unweakening until 4:45 A.M.

In a period of three hours and fifteen minutes, England had been smitten by the worst storm in its history. Damage ranged for miles.

Shacks and barns were blown off their foundations. Sturdy dwellings were left looking like skeletons. Chimneys and church spires collapsed. Tens of thousands of trees were knocked down. The streets of London lay covered with roof tiles.

Eight thousand persons were known to have lost their lives at sea. Ships littered the shore. In the Thames River alone sprawled a mass of seven hundred broken vessels.

More than fifteen thousand sheep drowned near Bristol, where sea walls crumbled. In places as far inland as twenty-five miles, the grass was so salty from the ocean wind that cattle refused to graze for many days.

Sunday morning the skies cleared; the storm had passed. People along the shore came out of their homes and looked toward the Eddystone Lighthouse. They looked in vain.

The lighthouse had vanished. There was not the slightest sign that it had ever existed! Eventually, at low tide, the retreating waters revealed a few twisted iron rods.

The great storm had brought death, suffering, and ruin to thousands—and to one man his proudest wish.

Now, in the calm morning air, Henry Winstanley's words seemed to hang like an echo above the twisted iron rods, all that remained of his lighthouse.

"I hope to be inside it during the greatest storm that ever blew under the face of heaven!"

He had got his wish.

He Saw over the Horizon

This is the story of a man who had a fantastic gift. He could foretell the approach of ships before they appeared on the horizon.

We do not know his first name. His last name was Bottineau, and he was French.

One day in 1762 he was looking out to sea when he noticed something that excited him. It seemed to him that a ship approaching land produced a certain effect on the atmosphere.

Bottineau made many observations during the months that followed. In the beginning, his record of "seeing" ships before they actually came into sight was discouraging. Sometimes he was right. More often he was wrong. For a time he gave up hope of success.

In 1764 he was appointed to a position on

Mauritius (at that time called Île de France), an island in the Indian Ocean. The move was a stroke of fortune.

The clear sky and pure atmosphere at Mauritius were more favorable to his studies than the coast of France. Also, there were fewer ships. He was less liable to be thrown off by vessels that sailed beyond the horizon without ever coming into sight.

As the years passed, he became so expert that he could foretell the day of a ship's arrival——one, two, three, or four days in advance——as well as the *number* of ships.

He called his discovery Nauscopie.

Between 1778 and 1782 he announced the arrival of 575 vessels before they became visible. He seldom missed. His errors were later proved to be vessels that did not touch at Mauritius, or else vessels delayed by contrary winds and currents.

Bottineau thought others could be taught Nauscopie. He made no secret of what must be learned.

The ocean, he explained, gives off gases due to the great number of dead animals, fishes, birds, and vegetables as well as minerals within it. When the water is disturbed by storms or the movement of a ship, the gases rise like smoke, making a kind of envelope around the ship. The envelope becomes visible when it meets other gases, like those surrounding another ship or escaping from land.

When the vessel sails with a fair wind and meets no obstacle, Bottineau asserted, the envelope moves swiftly and arrives several days before the vessel. Then the observer can announce the presence of a vessel at a considerable distance. But when the vessel meets with contrary winds, the envelope is influenced greatly. It sometimes appears four or five days before the vessel, and sometimes only a day.

After eighteen years on Mauritius, Bottineau took passage to France. He hoped to sell Nauscopie to the French government.

Aboard ship he continued his studies. He wanted to know if the effect on the atmosphere was the same when one ship approached another, and if he could discover land from a vessel.

Nauscopie worked under these new conditions. During the trip he predicted the approach of twenty-seven ships. He discovered land three times: once the captain denied the possibility, but upon checking his position, he admitted his error and changed course!

Arriving in France, Bottineau journeyed straight to Paris. He brought with him letters attesting to his ability from the governor of

Mauritius and the officers of the island's garrison.

Nevertheless, he was denied an audience. His claims were unacceptable to reason. Officials refused to see him.

Abbé Fontenay, editor of *Mercure de France,* heard of his "pretended" discovery. Without asking to see Bottineau's letters, Fontenay ridiculed him and insisted it was not "ships at sea, but castles in the air" that he had seen.

Bottineau despaired. "In this state the affair remains," he wrote. "All I can add is, that should vexation and disappointment end my life before I can explain my discovery, the world will probably be deprived for some time of an art that would have done honor to the eighteenth century."

Bottineau foretold his end truly. Disappointment brought on failing health. He died broken-hearted, unheard, and unhonored.

And Nauscopie died with him.

Ghost on the Quarterdeck

Something strange was going on aboard the U.S.S. *Constellation.*

Men who passed her berth at night reported hearing noises. Some even claimed to have seen misty shapes on her deck.

Was the historic old ship haunted?

A corvette of 176 feet, the *Constellation* was completed back in 1855, the last sailing man-of-war built for the United States Navy. She became a national heirloom. In September, 1954, she was put on display at Fort McHenry, Baltimore.

It was in Baltimore in 1955—a hundred years after her launching—that the strange disturbances were reported.

The reports reached Commander Allen Ross Brougham, executive officer at the nearby Na-

val Reserve Training Center. At first he regarded the affair lightly. At the same time, his
curiosity was aroused.

He got in touch with a friend whose hobby
was the supernatural and was expertly advised: the best time of year to see "ghosts" of
this type was at midnight during the period
between Christmas and New Year.

Commander Brougham selected Thursday
night. He mounted a camera overlooking the
quarterdeck and waited. At midnight it happened.

Something—a ghost?—appeared on the
quarterdeck wearing a fancy, old-fashioned
uniform. To Commander Brougham, the gold-
striped trousers, cocked hat, heavy gold epau-
lets, and sword looked like a uniform that
might have been worn by one of the *Constellation*'s captains.

An instant before the appearance, Commander Brougham had smelled something like
gunsmoke. Then, so suddenly that he barely
had time to click the shutter of his camera,
"it" vanished.

"It was all over in the time he took to take
a single stride," declared the commander. "I
was aware, somehow, that he was moving with
a great sense of urgency."

Commander Brougham's photograph shows

a cloudy figure reaching across his waist with his right hand, as if to draw his sword.

The picture was published on December 31, 1955, in the *Baltimore Sun,* accompanied by an article by feature writer Patrick Catling.

The most important part of the weird occurrence was not *who* the ghost was, according to Commander Brougham.

"The most important thing," he said, "is that the spirit of the old *Constellation* has shown itself in this dramatic fashion.

"You see," he went on, "it just happens that January is Naval Recruiting Month. And here we have a reminder from the Navy's past . . . that the Navy must always remain strong enough to defend freedom.

"It's a nice thought, isn't it?"

A Cargo of Death

In 1906, the world hailed the Norwegian sloop *Gjoa* as the first ship to navigate the treacherous Northwest Passage atop North America.

Since the sixteenth century seafarers had hunted for this fabled waterway linking the Atlantic and Pacific Oceans. The search through the frozen wastelands of the Arctic cost hundreds of lives and millions in treasure.

Now the Northwest Passage had been found and navigated. It proved a shorter route for trade between Europe and the Far East. The long haul around the bottom of South America became unnecessary.

The sturdy 70-foot *Gjoa* and her commander, Norwegian explorer Roald Amundsen, richly deserved the honors heaped upon them.

But old sailors shook their heads knowingly.

Amundsen and his six-man crew were *not* the first to sail through the Northwest Passage—they were the first to sail through alive.

There is a difference—and the difference is grim.

Over 130 years before the *Gjoa,* the Northwest Passage was conquered by the merchant-man *Octavius.* She never received the glory due her, for her horrifying triumph was witnessed only by the crew of the whaling ship *Herald.*

On August 12, 1775, the *Herald,* out of Greenland, was plowing the northern stretches of the Atlantic. She had weathered a storm the night before, and now her lookout scanned the landscape of icebergs for a safe channel.

Suddenly he spied masts poking up behind a low island of ice. "A ship!" he shouted. "A ship, west ahead!"

In half an hour the ship had swung clear of the iceberg and drifted slowly into the open water. The nearer she came, the more certain were the men of the *Herald* that something was terribly wrong.

She had the look of mystery and tragedy. Her sails hung in shreds. Ice coated her spars and rigging and glistened in the sunlight.

Captain Warren, master of the *Herald,* clapped a telescope to his eye. Vainly he sought signs of life.

"We'll board her," he announced. "Lower the longboat!"

His crew had small taste for the eerie stranger. But the order was obeyed. Captain Warren picked eight men to go with him.

As they approached the mystery vessel's stern, Captain Warren made out her name, faded and weather-beaten, but readable: *Octavius.*

No one in the longboat had heard of her. Muttering spread, but Captain Warren restored order with a sharp rebuke. He snapped out orders and climbed aboard, followed by four nervous and unhappy seamen.

The deck of the *Octavius* was covered with ice and crusted snow. The only sounds were the lazy creaking of the timbers and the whisper of the wind stirring in the rigging.

Captain Warren trudged to the forecastle. A thick shield of ice had to be knocked away before the entrance could be opened. The door swung, and a powerful, musty stench issued forth. The boarding party stepped inside, and stopped in their tracks.

Lying in bunks, bundled in clothes and

blankets, were twenty-eight frozen men—perfectly preserved by the deadly Arctic cold.

The captain's cabin was entered next. His body was seated at a table. By his hands lay a pen and the ship's log. Captain Warren entrusted the log to one of his men and continued to explore.

In an adjoining cabin was the body of a woman. She lay in her bunk on her side as if she had died watching something of keen interest.

In the center of the cabin was the body of a seaman, seated cross-legged. He held a flint in one hand and a piece of steel in the other. On the floor in front of him was a pile of wood scraps. Obviously he had frozen to death while attempting to light a fire.

A sailor's heavy jacket was beside the man. Captain Warren lifted it. Beneath lay the body of a young boy.

The men of the *Herald* wanted no more of the accursed ship. They dropped into the longboat and threatened to leave Captain Warren behind if he did not join them at once.

He demanded more time to investigate, but he could do nothing with men on the verge of panic. Furious but helpless, he returned to the *Herald*. The *Octavius* drifted away, never to be seen again.

Captain Warren took the log to his cabin. All but the first three pages and the last page had fallen out. The sailor to whom he had entrusted the book had been too frightened to notice the loss. Still, the four pages made it possible to piece together the ill-starred voyage.

The first three pages reported that the *Octavius* had sailed east from England bound for the China trade on September 10, 1761. On board were the captain, his wife, his ten-year-old son, and a crew of twenty-nine. The weather was good and the ship sighted the Canary Islands.

The last page was dated November 11, 1761, fourteen months later. It had but a single entry:

We have now been enclosed in the ice seventeen days. Our position is approximately Longitude 160 W, Latitude 75 N. The fire went out yesterday, and our [sailing] master has been trying to light it again, but without success. He has given the steel and flint to the mate. The master's son died this morning and his wife says she doesn't feel the terrible cold any longer. The rest of us seem to have no relief from the agony.

Captain Warren got out his charts and checked the figures. . . . Longitude 160 W, Latitude 75 N. He stared in disbelief.

On the day of the last entry, the *Octavius* was locked in ice north of Point Barrow, Alaska—on the *Pacific* side of North America. But when he had found her, she was drifting in the Atlantic! How did she get there?

One explanation only was possible.

On the homeward trip, the captain of the *Octavius* had apparently decided to find the Northwest Passage instead of sailing the long route around South America. Like so many before him, he had found death instead.

But the *Octavius* had continued the voyage. Year after year she had sailed eastward, her wheel unattended, her deck silently gathering layers of snow and ice. Year after year she had inched her way, beaten by storms and crunching ice. Blindly, haltingly, she had groped along the Northwest Passage, standing icebound in winter and drifting again with the spring thaw. Her stout hull had resisted and endured until she had won—won over all the forces that the Arctic could hurl against her—until she had floated at last upon the broad Atlantic.

One hundred and thirty years after the *Herald*'s discovery, the herring boat *Gjoa* passed through the same waters and brought fame to her commander, Roald Amundsen. Amundsen was a true hero. But the honor of being the first to conquer the Northwest Passage does not belong to him.

The honor belongs to the *Octavius*. For thirteen years the gallant ship had sailed on, carrying the frozen corpses of all aboard her.

Revenge of the Frigorifique

Does a ship have a mind and will of her own? Is there a shadowy life that never shows on a builder's blueprints, but which is born when sea and hull first touch together?

Common sense answers no. But what occurred on March 19, 1884, off the Brittany coast of France, answers *yes!*

A fog had closed visibility to a few feet. Most ships had stopped moving and were sounding fog signals or sirens. A few, like the French ship *Frigorifique*, were holding course, feeling their way at slow speed.

The *Frigorifique* was bound for Rouen from Pajajes, Spain. As she crept along, her crew heard a faint siren. In the sound-deadening fog, it was hard to tell how far away the other ship was, or in what direction.

Raoul Lambert, captain of the *Frigorifique,* ordered the engines stopped. He sounded three warning blasts on the siren. The crew listened. They heard nothing. Silent fog, like a heavy blanket, enclosed the ship.

The *Frigorifique* resumed speed at a careful four knots, her bell tolling ceaselessly. Suddenly a seaman at the cathead uttered a yell. "Ship to starboard!"

A black hull nosed out of the cottony swirls.

The *Frigorifique*'s steersman was unable to avoid a collision though he swung the helm hard to port. With a shrill wail of creaking and grinding, bulwarks crumpled. The *Frigorifique* reeled to port and came to a standstill, listing badly.

After a quick inspection, Captain Lambert ordered a lifeboat lowered. The *Frigorifique* was done for. Her eleven crewmen were taken aboard the other ship, the English collier *Rumney,* bound from Cardiff to La Rochelle.

Meanwhile, the abandoned *Frigorifique* disappeared into the fog.

The *Rumney* was undamaged and steamed on for two miles. Although the fog was as thick as ever, the rescued crew of the *Frigorifique* now felt safe. No one ever had been sunk twice in the same day. . . .

Suddenly the *Rumney*'s lookout shrilled, "Starboard! Ship to starboard!"

Out of the fog loomed a ship. She was making straight for the *Rumney!*

The steersman got the *Rumney* around, and the ships passed side to side. Neither ship was so much as scratched, and yet the rescued French crew stood rooted to the deck, gaping. They had seen the other ship clearly, and she was no stranger.

She was their own ship, the *Frigorifique.* Instead of being at the bottom of the ocean, she was still afloat and under steam.

Two miles later, the *Rumney*'s lookout again shouted a warning. The men on deck stared into the fog and saw the *Frigorifique* charging like a vengeful demon for the second time—silent, crewless, attacking. She did not miss.

The ships collided. Seawater poured into the *Rumney* while the *Frigorifique* slipped off into the fog triumphantly.

Before the *Rumney* went under, two lifeboats carrying the French and English crews pulled away. The men rowed toward land, and in thirty minutes came into clear daylight. They saw the dark line of the coast—and the *Frigorifique!* She was emerging from the edge of the fog, moving slowly on a wide, looping course.

The rowboats angled toward her and got alongside. Captain Lambert and five of his crew clambered aboard.

She was deserted. Captain Lambert found the ocean had not quite drowned the boilers. They had continued to work and drive the propellers after he had given the order to abandon ship.

Going to the helm, Captain Lambert saw the wheel lashed hard to port, as it had been left. That was the answer! The fixed wheel had guided the *Frigorifique* on a spiraling course that regularly crossed the path of the slower-moving *Rumney*.

Below him rose a deep, warning gurgle. The *Frigorifique* was in her death throes. But now Captain Lambert and his men waited until they were positive, until the deck was nearly swamped. Then they returned to the lifeboat.

Watching his ship bubble and sink, Captain Lambert's mind was eased. He had discovered the answer to the *Frigorifique*'s two passes at the *Rumney*—the first which had missed and the second which had sent the English ship under. The lashed wheel.

She had not sought revenge at all, Captain Lambert assured himself. Revenge is an emotion belonging to man. A ship is wood and iron and steel, nothing more.

Or is it?

Twice the *Frigorifique* had tried to sink the ship that had rammed her, succeeding on the second sweep. Fatally hurt herself, she had stayed afloat long enough to come back a *third* time; she had followed her crew out of the fog *as if to make certain they were all right.*

Then she had gone down, in peace.

Project Habakkuk

One of the best kept secrets of World War II was a plan for building an aircraft carrier nearly a mile long—almost entirely of *ice!*

The idea was thought up by the British in September, 1942. With such a floating air-field, planes could be refueled and kept over remote battle areas or guard against German submarines in mid-ocean.

The project, nicknamed Habakkuk, called for a man-made iceberg that resembled a standard aircraft carrier, only many times larger. The huge vessel was to be 5,000 feet long, 2,000 feet wide, and 100 feet high. She would run under her own power by means of motors fixed in caves in her hull. Cost of construction was set at $70 million.

Early experiments showed that natural ice

was too brittle for safe use. By adding wood pulp in several forms to ordinary sea ice, engineers got a mixture that was very tough. The new product was called Pykrete, in honor of its inventor, Geoffrey Pyke.

Lord Louis Mountbatten, Britain's Chief of Combined Operations, showed how tough it was. At a meeting of the Allied leaders in Quebec, Canada, he had two blocks of ice wheeled into the room. One block was common ice, the other was Pykrete.

Mountbatten invited the strongest man present to cut the blocks in half. General Henry A. Arnold, Commander of the United States Air Force, was elected. Mountbatten handed him a chopper.

Arnold split the common ice with a single blow. Smiling, he swung at the Pykrete. As the chopper hit, he cried out. His arms had been painfully jolted. The Pykrete was hardly scratched.

Mountbatten topped the show by drawing a pistol from his pocket. He shattered the common ice with one bullet. Then he fired at the Pykrete. The bullet bounced off, barely missing Sir Charles Portal.

During the winter of 1942–43, a small-scale model sixty feet long was secretly constructed at Patricia Lake in Alberta, Canada. The model successfully passed the test of summer heat. As the ice melted, the wood pulp quickly formed a furry coat which slowed the melting process. If needed, a small refrigerator plant was ready to keep the ice frozen.

British Prime Minister Winston Churchill was enthusiastic. The mile-long ships would be less costly and quicker to build than regular aircraft carriers. He foresaw "the use of two or three such refueling bases for an attack on Norway," and as stepping stones across the Bay of Bengal for an attack on Sumatra.

But the world's largest ice cubes were never built. By December, 1944, the menace of the German submarine fleet was greatly relieved. Conventional Allied warships had begun to win mastery of the seas.

So Project Habakkuk was shelved. Had it become a reality, it would have launched upon the oceans an aircraft carrier made of 35,000 square miles of ice and displacing a million tons. Hoisted upon her deck, the ordinary destroyer would have looked as tiny as a lifeboat.

The Bottle Post

Have you ever dreamed of finding a bottle on the shore, opening it, and reading a message of hope, despair, mystery, or romance?

Your chances are better than you think.

"Bottle post," the mail service of the seven seas, has been delivering amazing messages for centuries.

In the winter of 1956, Aarke Wiking, a lonesome young Swedish sailor, threw a bottle from his ship into the Mediterranean. Inside the bottle was a note asking any pretty girl aged sixteen to twenty to write to him.

Almost two years later, Sebastiano Puzzo, a factory worker, found the bottle on a beach in Sicily. He showed the note to his pretty daughter, Paolina, eighteen. As a joke, she wrote to

Wiking. An exchange of letters followed, and romance blossomed. In the fall of 1958, Paolina and Aarke were married.

Athough a bottle seems easily breakable, a message has no better carrier. Glass will last almost forever, and a sealed bottle is incredibly seaworthy. It will stay afloat through storms that sink large ships.

Divers in 1954 found eighteen bottles of beer in a ship sunk off the East Kent coast of England two hundred fifty years before. The beer was terrible, but the bottles were just fine.

The bottle post has an astonishing way of delivering a message to the right place. In 1924, Boyle Branscum placed a picture of himself wearing a basketball uniform inside a bottle and set it adrift in an Arkansas river. Twenty-five years later, the bottle was found by Bill Headstream on a beach near his home in Largo, Florida.

Headstream remembered the boy in the photo. As a return address was on the back of the picture, he wrote to Branscum. The two men had been boyhood friends when Headstream lived in Arkansas. They hadn't heard from each other until the bottle nudged ashore!

A bottle that drifted to Tasmania, Australia, in 1953 bore the names of two Australian soldiers on a troopship bound for France in 1916. The handwriting of one of the soldiers was recognized by his mother. He was killed in action in 1918, thirty-seven years before his message came into her hands.

More amazing still is the case of Chunosuke Matsuyma. A Japanese seaman, he started out in 1784 with forty-four shipmates to search for buried treasure. Their ship was wrecked on a coral reef, and all starved to death.

Before he died, Matsuyma scratched the story of the disaster onto a piece of wood, sealed it in a bottle, and cast it into the Pacific. The bottle wandered for one hundred fifty years. In 1935, it was picked up in Hiratuemura, the seaside village where Matsuyma was born!

Over the ages, the bottle post has performed all kinds of services for mankind. It has even carried state secrets. In the sixteenth century, Queen Elizabeth I of England made hanging the penalty for opening a message-carrying bottle. The duty belonged solely to her appointed official, the Court Bottle Opener.

Sometimes the seagoing post clears up the mystery of vanished ships. In November, 1933, the steamer *Saxilby* put out from Newfoundland for Port Talbot and simply disappeared.

Two years passed without a clue to the ship or her crew of twenty-nine.

Then one afternoon a cocoa tin washed ashore at Aberavon, a hamlet in Wales. The note inside solved the mystery: "S.S. *Saxilby* sinking somewhere off the Irish coast. Love to sister, brothers, and Dinah—Joe Okane."

Among the most tragic bottle messages is one written aboard the *Lusitania*. The ocean liner was torpedoed early in World War I and hundreds perished.

Many of the passengers used the little time left them to write notes to loved ones and tossed them into the onrushing sea. One note describes how it was in those last moments.

"I am still on deck with a few people. One is a child. The last boats have left. We are sinking fast. The orchestra is playing bravely. Some men near me are praying with a priest. The end is near. Maybe this note . . ."

There is no more. Apparently the writer had just enough time to seal the message in a bottle.

Not all bottles bear tales of tragedy however. Some bring treasure.

The David Jones department store of Sydney, Australia, marked its 120th anniversary in 1958 by releasing a bunch of bottles into the ocean. Each bottle held a note entitling the finder to a gift. The worth of the gifts totaled Australian £5,700, or about $12,500. Most are yet to be found.

Money mail—bottles with cash or checks inside—is often flung over the side by wealthy cruise passengers. After Charles Lindbergh's flight across the Atlantic in 1927, a tipsy American tourist dropped a bottle from the liner *President Roosevelt*. It contained a large check and the note: "Hurrah for Lindbergh!"

A French dressmaker discovered the bottle on the waterfront at Saffi, Morocco. To her surprise and delight, the check was perfectly good.

Bottles have long been used by scientists to trace ocean currents. The U.S. Navy each year turns loose thousands of sealed bottles in waters around the world.

Instructions in eight languages ask finders to fill out the enclosed forms with place and date of recovery. Some 350 forms come back each year and provide information for drawing current charts.

After both world wars floating bottles helped make sea-lanes safe. Thousands of deadly mines had gone adrift and menaced peacetime shipping. By studying the movements of the bottles, authorities determined where mines were most likely to be encountered—and avoided.

To encourage the return of these current finders, rewards are sometimes included in the bottles.

Bottles dropped off the southeast coast of Florida included coupons good for two dinners at one of Miami's better restaurants. In 1965, six-year-old Glenn S. Sobol of Miami found thirteen of the bottles on a beach in Key Biscayne. He treated his parents to a festival of dining out.

Today, all sorts of bottles—ketchup bottles, beer bottles, whiskey bottles—are bobbing around the world. They may wash up anywhere, including *your* beach.

Evidence from a Shark

The smuggling trade of the American merchantman *Nancy* came to an end because of a hungry shark!

On the morning of August 23, 1788, the *Nancy* was south of Haiti when the lookout spied a British man-of-war, the *Sparrow*. The *Nancy*'s captain and crew sprang into action.

The crew dumped overboard several crates of weapons, the illegal part of the cargo. The captain fed the ship's papers to the ocean. He had another, fake set to substitute in case of just such an emergency.

When the boarding party from the man-of-war arrived, the *Nancy* was clean. Nonetheless, she was taken to Port Royal, Jamaica.

Great Britain at this time was at war with Prussia, Holland, France, and Austria. British warships blockaded enemy ports in the West Indies to keep them from receiving supplies.

The British boarded any large ship that ventured into West Indian waters. Even ships of neutral nations, like the United States, were subject to search.

The master of the *Sparrow* insisted that the *Nancy* had been bringing weapons and stores to the Dutch in Curaçao. He wanted the merchantman seized as a prize of war.

The owners of the *Nancy* maintained that she was trading in neutral ports only. They demanded the release of their ship.

The Admiralty Court which heard the case found no evidence of smuggling. The Royal Navy was given a day to let the *Nancy* go or advance proof that she had been engaged in forbidden trade.

Before the deadline was up, the captain of another British warship, the *Abergavenny,* rushed panting into the Court of the Vice Admiralty. He carried the *Nancy*'s original papers.

The papers had been found that morning in the belly of a shark caught by his men!

The water-soaked bundle was dried out. The papers proved that the *Nancy* had been running the blockade to trade with Britain's enemies. Among the evidence was an order to the captain to put in at Curaçao, the Dutch port.

"The Shark's Papers" are today in the Institute of Jamaica at Port Royal. The shark's head is on exhibition in the Royal United Service Institution in London.

Who Fell Overboard?

On March 27, 1942, Task Force 39, commanded by Rear Admiral John W. Wilcox, Jr., departed Casco Bay, Maine, and headed across the Atlantic.

The force was to join a British fleet at Scapa Flow, Scotland. Together the ships of both nations would convoy transports through the sub-infested route to North Russia.

The American Navy was spread dangerously thin. Four months earlier, five battleships had been sunk and three others damaged at Pearl Harbor. Every ship, every man was desperately needed to fight the enemy.

Task Force 39 was the first American heavy unit sent into British waters in World War II. It consisted of two heavy cruisers, *Wichita* and *Tuscaloosa*, the aircraft carrier *Wasp*, eight destroyers, and Admiral Wilcox's flagship, the 45,000-ton battleship *Washington*.

Two days out of Maine, the zigzagging warships ran into foul weather. Lookouts wearing five thicknesses of wool inside sheepskin coats shivered in snow and freezing spray. Gale winds beat the ocean into lumpy mountains. The *Wasp*'s flight deck, fifty feet above the waterline, was awash.

Aboard the *Washington*, sharp eyes scanned the gray overcast and heaving seas, alert for an air attack or a torpedo sighting. At 10:30 A.M. came a blood-chilling cry—"*Man overboard!*"

The fantail lookout had spied a man in the battleship's foaming wake. The grim message blared over the telephone talker.

Captain H. H. J. Benson raced to the bridge at once. In seconds the *Washington*, bound by wartime radio silence, signaled the other ships with flags and whistles.

The *Tuscaloosa* and the destroyer *Livermore* peeled from formation and sped toward the flagship's stern. The *Tuscaloosa* signaled that she had seen a man in the water and had thrown him a life buoy. Soon afterward, the *Livermore*, too, reported seeing the man.

Neither ship, however, could recover him in the towering seas though they hunted for an hour.

Four search planes were launched by the *Wasp*. One splashed down and was lost. The others returned, without success.

Aboard the *Washington,* in the meantime, the question was being asked from bow to stern: Who had gone overboard?

Captain Benson ordered a roll call of every officer and sailor of the battleship's crew. It wasn't long before the answer reached the bridge, and it was astonishing.

Every man was present!

Captain Benson wondered if somehow there had been a mistake. But how? While no one had actually seen a man fall, six of the *Washington's* crew had seen him in the water. So had men of the *Tuscaloosa* and the *Livermore*.

He ordered a second roll call. This time each officer was told to check by sight every man on his roster. While the results were awaited, the *Washington* plowed on. The man, whoever he was, by now was beyond help.

The second roll call came up. It was the same as the first. No one was missing!

Somewhere, somehow, a costly error had been made. Two ships had broken formation. A search plane had been lost with its crew.

Two roll calls had wasted time and effort. A full report was sent to the admiral.

Admiral Wilcox was not in his cabin.

He was not anywhere aboard the ship. The truth was hard to believe. . . .

Only one man was not carried on the ship's roster—Admiral Wilcox himself. He was the missing man!

The freak accident that cost his life will never be known. He is the only United States admiral ever swept overboard at sea.

The Incredible Mistake

No book on strange sea happenings would be complete without the story of Sir George Tryon. On a hot, peaceful afternoon he gave the order that sent his battleships head-on to disaster.

It was June 22, 1893, and Britain's Mediterranean fleet was performing maneuvers on a glass-smooth sea. Watching from the bridge of the mighty *Victoria* was Vice Admiral Tryon. The flag flying from the masthead bore silent witness that he had gained the highest position in the Navy of his day—Commander-in-Chief of the Mediterranean Station.

A tall, heavy-set, bearded man, Admiral Tryon had risen to the top by sheer merit. Since 10 A.M. he had been putting the fleet through its paces, executing unusual and brilliant maneuvers for which he was famous.

He enjoyed the admiration of his country and the unquestioning loyalty of every man under him. His second-in-command, Rear Admiral A. H. Markham, trusted him blindly. Maurice Bourke, captain of the *Victoria,* later was to tell survivors to "do everything to preserve Sir George's reputation."

At 2:20 P.M. Admiral Tryon ordered the fleet formed into two parallel columns. The *Victoria* led the starboard column of six ships. Abreast of her, leading the remaining five ships, was Admiral Markham's flagship *Camperdown.*

For nearly an hour the fleet moved north by east, the two columns only 1,200 yards apart.

"Too close," thought Captain Noel of the battleship *Nile.* "There must be some error." At 2:55 P.M. he signaled, "Please repeat." The *Victoria* signaled a repeat.

The 1,200 yards between the two columns of ships was maintained.

Other captains had misgivings, too. But they had been schooled to obey without question. Besides, the day's maneuvers had gone beautifully. In a few minutes they expected the order that would swing the two columns south by east toward the anchorage at Tripolo Roadstead in Lebanon.

However, Captain Bourke of the *Victoria* was aghast. He already knew how Admiral Tryon intended to turn the ships. Bourke had tried to persuade Tryon to open the distance between the two columns to 1,600 yards.

Admiral Tryon at first had agreed; then he had insisted upon the original distance, 1,200 yards. Captain Bourke returned to the bridge, dumbfounded.

At 3:37 P.M. the flag lieutenant hoisted a pair of divisional signals. Rear Admiral Markham and Captain Johnstone saw them from the *Camperdown*. They stared in amazement.

The order to the fleet was fantastic. It would cause the ships of Admiral Tryon's column to turn, leading ships first, in a half circle toward Admiral Markham's column. Markham's column, like a mirror image, would turn in toward Admiral Tryon's.

"It can't be done," muttered Captain Johnstone.

Admiral Markham snapped, "Send back, 'Signal not understood.'"

Before the message could be completed, the *Victoria* signaled again: "What are you waiting for?"

Obediently, Captain Johnstone put the *Camperdown* into a turn.

If the two columns were farther apart, the maneuver would have been sensational—and possible.

However, neither the *Victoria* nor the *Camperdown,* two of Britain's largest battleships, could make a half circle in less than 600 yards. With only 1,200 yards between them, they would collide!

Officers of the fleet were stunned. Seeking wildly for an explanation, they decided the commander-in-chief had something up his sleeve—a clever maneuver that would clear up the mess.

Slowly, like two sightless giants, the *Victoria* and the *Camperdown* swung toward each other. . . .

Captain Custance of the cruiser *Phaeton* had seen nothing wrong with the signal. "That gives me two cables to turn in," he had thought. Then suddenly he realized that he had mistaken the radius of the fleet's turning circle for its diameter. Had the admiral done the same?

In all probability, yes. Tryon had tried the same maneuver in 1890, three years before. One of his better captains, seeing the danger, had flown the repeat-hoist at the dip and stubbornly kept it there. The admiral had called off the maneuver, avoiding a collision.

The *Victoria* and the *Camperdown* steadily closed on each other. Tension mounted. Up and down the two columns men waited in numb, horrified silence.

Was Admiral Tryon thinking back to three years ago? Was he determined to prove that the maneuver, called off then, would work?

Captain Bourke was on the verge of ordering the engines of the *Victoria* reversed on his own responsibility—an act of mutiny—when word came from Admiral Tryon. "Full astern, port engine!"

Captain Bourke relayed the command. Moments later he ordered *both* engines reversed.

It was too late.

With a scream of rent steel, the battleships collided. The *Camperdown*'s ram pierced the *Victoria*'s side. For a minute the two ships stayed locked together. Then the *Camperdown* pulled free. A gaping hole laid the *Victoria* open to the sea.

Admiral Tryon stood expressionless, dazed. "It's all my doing . . . all my fault," he whispered.

Ten minutes later the *Victoria* went down,

bow first. Admiral Tryon was trapped in the chart house by the crush of debris.

The other ships launched rescue boats. Among the 300 survivors was Captain Bourke.

But 358 men had lost their lives.

Why?

Because of an incredible blunder. The finest admiral in the British Navy had made a simple—and frightful—error in mathematics.

And he had paid for it with his life.

The Seagoing Coffin

Until the Civil War, no submarine had ever sunk an enemy warship. The chance to be the first was given to the South's *H. L. Hunley*.

In her test runs the *Hunley* showed both strength and weakness. She could dive and travel under water; that was her strength. Her weakness? She often didn't come up.

Hers was a grim habit of drowning crew after crew—her own.

Brave men continued to risk their lives in the seagoing coffin because the war was going badly for the South. The North had a mighty navy blockading the southern coasts and waterways. President Jefferson Davis had urged the citizens to help in the fight on the sea. His government agreed to pay, and pay handsomely, for every Northern man-of-war sunk.

Out of the double motives of profit and patriotism had come the *Hunley*.

Starting with an iron boiler about twenty-five feet long and four feet wide, her builders had set about making a submarine in Mobile, Alabama. They soon ran out of funds and had to appeal to outsiders. Horace L. Hunley put up the most fresh money, and for him the submarine was named.

In the summer of 1863 the *Hunley* was moved by two railroad flatcars to Charleston, South Carolina. The port city was blockaded. Here, among the Northern ironclads and wood ships, was a happy hunting ground for the South's new weapon.

A crew was enlisted under John Payne, an Army lieutenant. As Payne prepared to close the forward hatch for a shakedown run, a steamer passed close by. Her swell flooded the low-riding *Hunley*. Payne scampered to safety as the submarine sank with several of her crew.

Payne got permission to try again. The *Hunley* was raised and repaired. On her very next test, she went to the bottom. Payne and two crewmen escaped.

By now probably fourteen men had been drowned in the seagoing coffin. Yet she got another chance. From Mobile hurried Horace

L. Hunley, bringing his own crew. He insisted his namesake was sound.

On October 15 he proved himself in error. He and his men got into the submarine, dived, and never came up alive.

By all that makes sense, the *Hunley* should have remained in her watery grave to kill no more. But two engineers, Lieutenants George E. Dixon and William A. Alexander, raised the craft. They had helped design her, and they believed they could make her work.

In the following weeks, the *Hunley* seemed to have shaken the habit of sinking. She was taken out six and seven miles. But rough seas forced her to turn back without using her torpedo. A copper cylinder holding ninety pounds of explosive, the torpedo was fixed to a spar at the bow.

November and December dragged by. Toward the close of January, 1864, Alexander had to return to Mobile. Dixon stayed on at Charleston, waiting for ideal conditions—a dark and calm night.

On the evening of February 17, the wind died down and the sea calmed. A bright moon shone, however. The impatient Dixon decided to go out even though the moonlight might reveal the *Hunley* to the enemy.

The crew entered by the front and back

hatches and took seats at the ship-long propeller shaft. They gripped levers set in the shaft and waited for the order to begin cranking the propeller.

Dixon made the sub tight and let water into the ballast tanks. The *Hunley* settled three inches below water level. The second officer took his seat and the cranking began.

Dixon turned the lever which operated the fins. The *Hunley* dived. Driven by muscle power, she slid through the water at top speed, four knots. A mercury gauge showed the depth, but the sub lacked a periscope. Dixon's only view to the outside was through small glass panels set in the hatch.

Shortly before nine o'clock, Acting Master J. K. Crosby was standing on the deck of the North's sloop of war *Housatonic.* He saw a ruffle in the moonlit water a hundred yards away.

At first he thought it was a large fish or plank. But the thing came straight on. Word of the *Hunley* had been leaked to the North by a Southern deserter. Crosby sounded the alarm.

The *Housatonic* cast her moorings. With engines reversing, she backed smack into the *Hunley,* which had suddenly changed course.

The blast knocked sailors of the *Housatonic*

flat. The entire ship seemed to blow apart. Amazingly, all save five of her crew were rescued.

And the *Hunley*?

Years later she was discovered on the bottom, lying with her bow toward the wreck of the *Housatonic*. She had perished in the explosion, drowning the last of her brave crews.

But the seagoing coffin had written a page in naval warfare. Never before had an underwater craft sunk a warship. Not for fifty years would another submarine repeat the feat.

Across the Atlantic– by Rowboat!

It was a wild idea. Absolutely crazy!

George Harbo believed that if somebody rowed across the ocean, he could make a fortune. People would flock to see the boat—at twenty-five cents a head admission.

One man alone couldn't make it. But two had a good chance, Harbo figured. He took on a partner, Frank Samuelson.

Both men were Norwegians who had settled in Brooklyn, New York. Both were tired of dredging oysters off New Jersey for a living. They were still young: Harbo was thirty, Samuelson was twenty-six. Years at sea had made them strong, hardy, and poor.

Harbo had the details worked out. The best way to row was west to east. Thus, they could use the natural currents of the Gulf Stream and the North Atlantic Drift, which move in the direction they were going.

In addition, this route was heavily used by shipping. In case of trouble there would be help.

Working in their spare time for two years, the two men built a boat of white oak at Branchport, New Jersey. Pointed at both ends, she was eighteen feet long and five feet wide, with a draft of eight inches.

Into her went a compass, sextant, anchor, an air mattress, signal lights, and five gallons of kerosine for the tiny stove fitted into the bow. She carried five sets of oars, but no sails.

Harbo and Samuelson named her the *Fox,* after Richard K. Fox, publisher of the sporty *National Police Gazette.* Fox had put up the money though he privately thought the pair was committing suicide. He counted on getting heaps of publicity for his weekly no matter what happened.

On the morning of June 6, 1896, the two adventurers made ready to shove off. They stowed on board nine pounds of coffee, one hundred pounds of sea biscuits, two hundred fifty eggs, and plenty of canned meat. Except for oilskins, they took only the clothing they wore.

At 10 A.M. they stroked away from the Battery in lower New York City. The crowd of well-wishers numbered less than two thousand, and Richard K. Fox was beside himself with disgust and disappointment. The daily newspapers had given the event but passing mention, believing it a hoax. The *New York Times* had ignored the two Norwegians completely.

The *Fox* skimmed down the bay with both men rowing, singing, and dreaming of great wealth. Once land had faded into the distance, they settled down to their routine. This called for each of them to spend sixteen hours a day at the oars, sometimes alone, sometimes together.

The first few days were easy, despite the stove, which kept blowing out. Harbo and Samuelson resigned themselves to cold coffee and raw eggs.

The night of June 15 brought the first bad weather. An easterly gale battered the frail craft. Merely to hold their own, the Norwegians had to row at top speed. Finally, exhausted, they threw out the anchor. When the gale lifted, Harbo figured they had been blown backward thirty miles.

A shark bumped the boat and stalked behind for two days. The killer of the deeps was not so much trouble as passing ships, however.

Harbo and Samuelson had constant difficulty convincing captains that they were not shipwrecked sailors and did not want to be rescued. The *Fox* was manned by two sane men rowing to France.

On July 7, thirty-one days out of New York, a fierce storm overturned the boat. Harbo and Samuelson were prepared. Harbo had fastened handholds in the keel for just such an emergency.

Keeping their heads and using the handholds, they righted the *Fox,* an impossible feat but for her double-end construction. After an hour they had her bailed out. They fell to the oars once again.

They had lost much food. Wind, sun, and saltwater stung their flesh. Their hands were masses of blisters, and rowing became an agony. But half the voyage lay behind them.

Having done its worst without stopping them, nature now smiled. Favored by following winds and calm seas, the pair averaged seventy miles a day. On August 1, Samuelson sighted land. It was the Scilly Islands on the southwestern corner of Great Britain.

They touched shore at St. Mary's and then made for Le Havre, France, 250 miles away. There they ended their voyage, having rowed 3,200 miles.

The ordeal left them crippled. It was a week before either could stand. Their hands never fully recovered.

Harder to bear was the failure of the *Fox* to make them rich. In France, England, and Norway people paid admission to see the little boat. The income, however, barely paid expenses.

The *Fox* was brought home to America aboard an ocean liner. Here, too, she proved a flop. Few people had ever heard of her. Fewer still believed a word of what the barker said outside the exhibition tent. As a carnival attraction, a beat-up rowboat was less interesting than a two-headed calf or a pretty Egyptian dancer.

Crushed by the indifference of the public, Harbo and Samuelson went back to their oyster nets.

Nothing is known of Harbo thereafter. Samuelson eventually returned to his native Norway. In 1946 he died penniless in an old people's home.

The Missing Destroyer

During the course of World War II the United States Navy lost several ships whose exact fate was not immediately learned.

By the time the Japanese surrendered, however, all these ships had been accounted for—except one.

She was the *Edsall*, or *D.D. 219*. An outdated four-stack destroyer, she was more than twenty years old when fighting broke out. In March, 1942, three months after Pearl Harbor, she vanished into the Pacific somewhere off Java.

Navy records listed her as "missing in action." In other words, no one knew just what had happened to her and her crew of 153 American sailors.

Two clues found after the war only deepened the puzzle.

The bodies of five crewmen were discovered in a Japanese prisoner-of-war camp at Kendari in the Celebes. How they got there still stands as an unsolved mystery.

The logs of two Japanese battleships, the *Hiei* and the *Kirishima,* revealed that both ships claimed to have sunk her.

Years passed, and the *Edsall* remained on the record as "missing in action." The unwritten question mark hovering after her name began fading from memory.

Then, in 1952, Douglas Wood entered the Naval Photographic Center in Anacosta, Maryland, where the Navy stores films captured from the Japanese. Wood's job was to select footage for a planned television series, *Victory at Sea.*

One day he was sitting relaxedly in the projection room when suddenly he tensed, eyes riveted on the screen. What he saw was no phony propaganda film or newsreel for the home front.

The film had been taken from aboard a Japanese cruiser during a naval battle. The picture was shaky and constantly jumping about, as if the cameraman was in a state of high excitement.

The cruiser was firing salvo after salvo at an overmatched American destroyer. Before the sixty feet of battle strip sped through the projector, Wood saw the destroyer go down stern first.

Experts were called in. Individual movie frames were blown up to eight-by-ten-inch still pictures. The movie and the stills were studied over and over. After two months, there was no doubt.

It was the *Edsall,* probably sunk by the Japanese cruiser *Ashigara,* which in turn was later sunk by a British submarine. The confusion over which warship had fired the killing shot into the old four-stacker was blamed on the frenzy of the sea battle.

Ten years and ten thousand miles away, the case of the missing destroyer was solved. Thanks to an alert observer, the question mark was erased and a cloud lifted.

The *Edsall,* an aged leftover from prewar days, had died fighting against hopeless odds.

Arctic Wanderer

She was built by the Hudson Bay Company, and from the time she was launched in 1921, the *Baychimo* proved her ability to survive.

Her route tested every rivet and plate in her steel hull. From her home port of Vancouver, she steamed up the west coast of Canada, around Alaska, and entered the shipwrecking waters of the Northwest Passage. Calling at eight Hudson Bay Company trading posts, she dropped off supplies and took on bundles of furs.

For nine years the *Baychimo* visited Canada's northwest territories. No other ship had made the run for more than two years in a row.

She was tough. Just how tough, her builders never imagined.

In July, 1931, the *Baychimo* started north

on what was fated to be her last manned voyage. Before reaching the Northwest Passage, she encountered threatening weather. One of the harshest winters on record was awaiting her.

She met harder and harder going through thickening polar pack ice and fell behind schedule. On October 1, she stopped altogether, caught fast in an offshore ice field eighty miles from Wainright, Alaska. A million dollars' worth of furs lay in her hold.

Her skipper, Captain John Cornwall, radioed for help. On October 15, two planes of the Northern Air Transport circled above the helpless ship and landed on the ice. The pilots, Vic Ross and Hans Mirrow, had flown their small monoplanes over six hundred miles of some of the worst areas of the earth.

The pilots made three daring trips, taking twenty-two men to Nome. Captain Cornwall and fourteen of his crew stayed behind. They hoped the *Baychimo*'s hull could withstand the ice until the spring thaw, when she could be moved.

Captain Cornwall and his men brought materials from the ship and built a cabin on the shore a mile from the trapped vessel. They had a stove and lived well enough on canned food.

Early in November a gale struck. It raged for three days, during which the men were imprisoned in the cabin. When at last they set foot outside, they looked through the eerie polar twilight toward the *Baychimo*. She was gone—probably sunk or buried under tons of ice and snow.

Captain Cornwall and his men tramped along the frozen coast to the settlement of Point Barrow. There they were picked up by pilots Ross and Mirrow in March, 1932. Everyone agreed the *Baychimo* was by now lying at the bottom of the ocean. The Hudson Bay Company wrote her off as a total loss.

They were wrong. The *Baychimo* was very much alive.

During the gale she had snapped her cables and floated away. Christened by howling winds, she had launched herself on a new career—wanderer.

As if she had felt the hand of man too long, she has remained on her own ever since. Year after year she has followed a roaming course. Like some wild beast let loose to freedom, she has thwarted all efforts to bring her back to captivity.

In July, 1932, Eskimo hunters led by Joe Togtoq found her nearly fifty miles southwest of where Captain Cornwall had abandoned her. The Eskimos removed all the furs their dog teams could pull. They returned the following day for another load, but the *Baychimo* had other ideas. She had vanished.

During the next few years she was sighted time and again along the Alaskan coast by prospectors, Eskimos, whalers, and trading vessels.

In the summer of 1933, a party of Eskimo seal hunters spotted her northwest of Point Barrow. They put out in kayaks. Hardly had they got aboard when they were lashed by a blizzard, which they swore the *Baychimo* had summoned. After being stranded eleven days, five of the Eskimos drowned on the paddle back to shore.

A year afterward, the Canadian schooner *Trader* spied her. It was late in the afternoon, and the captain decided to remove what was left of her cargo the next day. The *Baychimo* was not made fast to the schooner—a mistake. During the night she drifted off. When dawn broke, she was beyond the horizon, wandering free once more.

Since then she has been occasionally seen by Arctic explorers, weather ships, and United States Air Force planes flying to Greenland. The most recently reported sighting was made in 1967 by Andrei Bruloff, master of the Russian trawler *Shelyagin.*

Like other seamen who know the Arctic waters, he marveled at her ability to survive.

"She is like no other derelict I have seen or heard of," he observed. "She acts as though she has a will of her own."

Since 1931, the *Baychimc* has defied the polar storms and slipped the ruinous traps of pack ice. A ghostly ship, she disappears for months and even years on end. Then, as if gaining in cunning, she shows herself long enough to make a game of tempting would-be captors.

Alone and untroubled by human hands, she still sails the far reaches of the north, proudly going her own mysterious way.

The Jinxed Ocean Liner

In the middle of the last century a wonder was fashioned in a London shipyard on a muddy strand of the Thames River.

It was the *Great Eastern,* a colossal steamship 692 feet long.

Fully loaded, the *Great Eastern* outweighed the 179 English ships that fought the great naval battle against the Spanish Armada in 1588.

She had two power plants. One drove a pair of 58-foot paddle wheels, each larger than a circus ring. The other drove a 24-foot propeller, which in sheer size has never been matched. She had four funnels and six masts, more than any other ship in history.

A floating city, she was designed to carry four thousand passengers, nearly twice as many as the *Queen Mary,* pride of Britain's twentieth century transatlantic fleet.

Beginning in May, 1854, two thousand men toiled a thousand working days to complete her hull. Before her launching, she gave no hint of being jinxed.

On the contrary, her builders took pride in the low casualty rate during construction. There was, however, a chilling rumor about a missing basher and his helper.

Bashers worked in teams hammering, or bashing, rivets. Two bashers stood outside and hammered at rivets held in place by a third, inside the hull. The inside basher was helped by three boys.

One boy minded the forge, another passed the heated rivet, and the third fitted the red-hot rivet into the hole. The men and the three boys sweated in the space between the double hulls twelve hours a day.

One morning a basher and his helper didn't show up for work and were never seen again. The rumor started: the missing pair had been accidentally sealed up, their cries lost in the hellish noises of more than a hundred hammers.

On November 3, 1857, a crowd estimated to be a hundred thousand lined the Thames River to see the launching. They witnessed instead a day of failure, panic, injuries, and the death of two men. The launching had to be called off.

Three months later another attempt was made—and succeeded. With no visitors present, the heaviest object ever moved by man rode her two cradles into the river.

"She's afloat!" shouted her captain, William Harrison, from the railing. "She's afloat!"

Two days before she departed for America, the man who designed her, Isambard Kingdom Brunel, made his final inspection. He was never to see her sail. Worry and overwork brought on a stroke. He collapsed on deck and died nine days later.

The *Great Eastern* began her maiden voyage on September 7, 1859. As she passed Hastings, her forward funnel blew off, killing five firemen. Nevertheless, she set a speed record for the Atlantic crossing.

She arrived in New York City to a hero's welcome. A hundred and forty-three thousand persons each paid a dollar admission to tour her. They stole everything not tied down and spat tobacco juice on everything else.

A sightseeing cruise around New York ended in a near mutiny of the passengers, who nearly starved for lack of food. Fights broke out among the crew. Two sailors were killed and thirteen injured in the brawls.

Three months after her first crossing, Captain Harrison, the coxswain, and the son of the purser drowned when their small boat overturned as they were going ashore. Harrison was replaced by John Vine Hall, who had suffered a nervous breakdown after the maiden voyage.

Forgotten were the missing basher and his young helper. They might well have been remembered. A jinx ate at the *Great Eastern* all her life.

She blew boilers, smashed paddles, lost masts, and collided with other ships. Altogether, she sank or damaged ten vessels.

She couldn't pay for herself. She never carried enough freight to fill her hold. Passengers sailed on other ships rather than risk injury aboard her. One crossing was made with 35 passengers and 418 crew members, including 3 doctors.

She cost about $5 million to build, and she ruined a parade of backers. Early in 1864, she was sold for $125,000. The amount was about a third of the sum it had cost to repair her hull after she had hit a rock pile in Long Island Sound in 1862.

She did gain some fame which was based neither on her size nor her jinx. She laid three cables across the Atlantic. But in 1874 she was replaced by the *Faraday,* which was built especially for cable laying.

The *Great Eastern* was brought back to England, where no one knew what to do with her. For a while she served as a showboat with advertisements painted on her hull and funnels. Thirty-one years after her launching, she was broken up for scrap.

Wreckers were busy one day when a shriek stopped work. Tools were dropped. Everyone came running to a compartment on the port side.

Trapped inside were the skeletons of the basher and his boy helper.

The Real Robinson Crusoe

The real-life model for Daniel Defoe's famous novel *Robinson Crusoe* was Alexander Selkirk, a young seaman with a mind of his own.

During the four years he spent stranded on a Pacific island, he danced with cats and goats to conquer his loneliness. He avoided capture by hostile Spaniards, outwitted rats, and cheated death in a tumble from a cliff. When he was rescued, he had almost forgotten how to speak.

Selkirk was born in 1676, the son of a god-fearing Scottish shoemaker. As a youth, he was quick-tempered, independent, and full of mischief. Trouble over his conduct at church caused him to run off to sea twice. The first time he stayed away six years, the second time for good.

In 1703, he sailed from England with Captain William Dampier's buccaneering expedition. Dampier had two ships, which were fitted out to prey upon French and Spanish merchantmen returning from South America and the West Indies loaded with treasure. Dampier appointed Selkirk first mate aboard the *Cinque Ports*.

While at sea, Selkirk fell out with his captain, Thomas Stradling. In Stradling's opinion, Selkirk's freely voiced criticisms bordered on mutiny. He bided his time.

In September, 1704, the *Cinque Ports* called at Juan Fernández, a group of small uninhabited islands off the coast of Chile. Stradling dispatched a longboat to pick up two sailors who had been accidently left behind on an earlier visit.

Selkirk unwisely chose that moment to be outspoken. He swore that he would rather stay on Juan Fernández than serve another day aboard the leaky *Cinque Ports*. Stradling gladly obliged him. In the days of piracy, it was not an uncommon practice to dump mutineers on a deserted island. Within an hour, Selkirk found himself on one of the Juan Fernández islands with all his belongings.

Standing alone on the beach, he underwent a change of heart. The realization of what he had brought upon himself overwhelmed him. He pleaded to be taken back. Stradling refused.

The *Cinque Ports* sailed away. Selkirk was abandoned to the company of goats, wild cats, crabs, seabirds, and rats.

For the first eight months his life was filled with the terror of being alone. He ate only when hungry and fell asleep watching the horizon. But he was intelligent, healthy, and young. The seafarer in him was used to hardships. A lesser man might have broken. Selkirk adapted.

Captain Stradling had left him with his clothes, bedding, a gun, one pound of powder, bullets, tobacco, a hatchet, a knife, a Bible, his mathematical instruments, and a few books. He made the most of them.

Out of pimento trees he built two huts and roofed them over with long grass. The walls he lined with the skins of goats, which abounded on the island. The goats, like the rats and cats, had been brought over by ships putting in for wood and water.

In the smaller hut Selkirk dressed the meat he had slain. He built the larger hut some distance away, and here he slept, read, sang psalms, and prayed. Later he was to declare that he was a better Christian while marooned than he had ever been, or than he should ever be again.

He made fires by rubbing two pimento sticks on his knee and used pimento logs for cooking and light. The logs burned with almost no smoke and gave off a refreshing odor.

In the beginning he caught fish, but they disagreed with him. Thereafter, he ate no seafood except crawfish, which were as big as lobsters and very good. He broiled or boiled them, as he frequently did with goat's meat to make broth.

Altogether, he killed five hundred goats while on the island. When his powder gave out, he developed a substitute: speed of foot.

According to one of his rescuers:

He ran with a wonderful swiftness through the woods and up the Rocks and Hills, as we perceived when we employed him to catch Goats for us. We had a Bull-Dog, which we sent with several of our nimblest Runners to help him catching Goats, but he distanced and tired both the Dog and the Men, caught the Goats, and brought them to us on his back.

Pursuing goats wore out his shoes. Forced to do without them, his feet toughened till he could run anywhere barefooted. After his rescue, it was some time before he could wear shoes again without having his feet swell up.

Some of the goats he ate and others he kept for milk and pets. With a nail for a needle, he stitched clothing from their skins, using thongs cut from the skins. When his knife and hatchet gave out, he made others from iron barrel hoops picked up along the shore. He pounded them thin with stones and sharpened them upon the rocks.

Goats formed the chief resource of his existence, providing him with food, clothing, and shelter. And yet it was a goat that nearly took his life.

He had chased it into some bushes, forgetting in his eagerness that the bushes concealed the brink of a cliff. Over and down went man and goat. Selkirk was knocked unconscious. When he came to his senses, he found the goat dead beneath him. He lay there twenty-four hours, bruised and aching, before he managed to crawl the mile to his hut. He did not stir outside for ten days.

To vary his diet of goat's meat and crawfish, he ate turnips, which Captain Dampier's men had planted and which had overspread several acres. He also ate the leaves of cabbage trees and spiced his meat with the pepperlike fruit of pimento trees.

Rats were at first a serious nuisance. They raided his food stocks and gnawed at his feet and clothes while he slept. He solved the problem by feeding goat's meat to the island's cat population. With hundreds of cats padding about his hut night and day, he was soon delivered from the rats.

To amuse himself and occupy the time, he often danced with the cats and pet goats and sang to them. Each morning he carved the date on a tree and hunted new trees on which to cut his name.

Twice he had visitors.

On the first occasion two ships anchored in the bay. Selkirk raced to the beach in welcome, but recognized the newcomers to be Spaniards. He wheeled and fled inland. Upon his sudden retreat, the Spaniards opened fire and started in pursuit.

Had they been Frenchmen, Selkirk might have surrendered. But the Spanish would guard the presence of their treasure ships in the area either by murder or by making him a slave in the mines. He feared them more than dying alone on the island.

He sprinted into the woods and hid in the top of a tall tree. Scarcely daring to draw breath he watched the Spaniards searching the ground below. They stopped at the foot of his tree, killed a few goats, and went off without spying him.

On February 2, 1709, two English privateers under Captain Woodes Rogers beached longboats. Four years and four months after Selkirk had been left on Juan Fernández, rescue had come.

The landing party was shocked to see coming toward them a single bronzed and bearded figure in goatskins. It was Selkirk. He had gone so long without speaking to another human being that he stammered and stuttered his joy, "speaking his words in halves."

Selkirk resumed his career as if it had never been interrupted. William Dampier, his old commander, was captain of one of the privateers and took him on as mate.

The two English ships attacked and captured several Spanish galleons. Before the year ended, Selkirk was given command of one of them. In 1710, while commanding another Spanish prize, he arrived in England.

Captain Woodes Rogers penned an account of the buccaneering expedition. Published in 1712 under the title *A Cruising Voyage Around the World,* the book included Selkirk's story. About the same time a catchpenny pamphlet appeared—*Providence Displayed, or a Surprising Account of one Alexander Selkirk ... Written by His Own Hand*. That Selkirk really wrote it himself is doubtful.

The Rogers book was reviewed in the widely read journal, *The Englishman*. Selkirk's adventures on Juan Fernández received the bulk of attention.

It was from this review that Daniel Defoe probably drew the inspiration for his fictional work, *Robinson Crusoe*. He may also have spoken with Selkirk, but that is unproved.

Robinson Crusoe was published on April 25, 1719. Selkirk lived long enough to see the world's imagination captured by the tale of the lonely island dweller.

He died in his forty-fifth year while serving as mate on the *Weymouth*. The entry in the ship's paybook is starkly indifferent to the man whose courage, strength, and common sense formed the basis for one of the most popular books ever printed.

Beside his name was noted only: "Dead, 12th Dec. 1721."

Some Called It Murder

On March 12, 1841, the *William Brown,* an American square-rigger, raised anchor and sailed from Liverpool, England. She picked her way down the Mersey River and set course for Philadelphia.

Misfortune stalked her almost as soon as she gained the open sea. Three times winds ripped every yard of her canvas to tatters. Almost every day for an entire month, unseasonable fogs wrapped around her. Cautiously she poked along under shortened sail.

Toward the evening of April 19, five weeks out of Liverpool, a decided chill announced the nearness of icebergs. An extra lookout went aloft, but the fog was too heavy for a thousand eyes. A few minutes before midnight, the *William Brown* crunched into an iceberg.

Captain George L. Harris and his first mate, Francis Rhodes, dashed below. They saw immediately that the ship was beyond saving. A gash seven feet high had been ripped in her bow. Rhodes ordered the ship's two lifeboats launched.

Up on deck, several of the fourteen-man crew were already fumbling to free the longboat. The passengers—sixty-five Scottish and Irish immigrants routed from sleep and but half-dressed—stampeded up from steerage. Their terrified shrieking and scuffling, combined with the yawing of the unmanageable vessel, created a scene of frenzied confusion.

Forty-one people charged into the longboat as she was being lowered. Only six or seven scrambled aboard the small jolly boat, which, swinging from the stern, was all but overlooked.

The two lifeboats, tied together, drew away from the schooner. Members of the crew pulled hard on their oars to get clear of the undertow when the ship went down. From twenty feet away, the *William Brown* was only a blurred outline in the darkness and fog.

The voices of the thirty-one men and women left behind on deck carried across the water. For half an hour their pleas and screams tormented the passengers crowded in the two boats. Then the pitiable chorus was drowned by a hideous gurgling. The *William Brown* had sunk into the North Atlantic.

Surrounded by icebergs, the two lifeboats drifted through the night, 250 miles from the nearest land. At first light, the fog lifted.

Captain Harris in the jolly boat called over to Rhodes, "I'm going to cut loose and try to make Newfoundland. You'd better do the same."

Rhodes, in command of the longboat, did not reply to the captain's words. Instead, he spoke on another subject, which obviously had been troubling him all night.

"We're badly overloaded. Can you take some of our people?"

"I'm sorry," the captain replied. "We're overloaded, too."

"We don't have sails," Rhodes pressed on. "We've several leaks, and the boat is so low in the water I'm afraid she'll swamp." The first mate paused, as if his next words were almost too heavy to utter. "We may have to do something—do you understand?"

The captain's voice was tight. "Yes."

"Do you agree?"

After a lengthy silence, the captain answered, "Only . . . if it *must* be done, Rhodes."

The mysterious conversation was lost on the passengers huddling in the longboat. But Rhodes seemed relieved, as if some dreadful weight had been lightened by sharing it with the captain.

Shouts of "Good luck!" and "God be with you!" were exchanged as Captain Harris leaned over and cut the rope. The two boats floated apart.

Sleet began to fall, adding to the water that seeped into the longboat from a score of leaks. Constant bailing was necessary. Hour after hour, Rhodes, seated by the tiller, stared strangely at his cargo of shivering, frightened humanity. At last he summoned Alexander Holmes, a member of the crew.

Young, strong, and intelligent, Holmes was a man for emergencies. Since the two lifeboats had separated, he had slowly taken over. He had directed the bailing, divided the meager food supply, and supervised whatever had to be done for comfort and safety.

Rhodes and Holmes whispered to each other, watched uneasily by every passenger. The meaning of the earlier conversation between Rhodes and Captain Harris dawned on them. The boat was dangerously overloaded. Part of the cargo had to be dumped.

Rhodes wasn't the man for it. He seemed stunned by the situation, unable to act——or unwilling. Holmes filled in. He signaled to James Murray, a powerful black seaman.

"Come on," said Holmes. "Let's get it over with."

They moved toward the bow where Owen Riley, a passenger, was lying. Holmes ordered him to stand up.

"Isabelle, help me!" Riley begged Mrs. Edgar, another passenger. When she didn't answer, he appealed to the others. The boat was hushed.

Holmes grabbed Riley and flung him over. There was a splash of frigid water. Riley's screams mingled briefly with those of the women in the boat. Then he vanished.

Holmes and Murray next advanced on George Duffee. He shrank back in terror. "I've got a wife and three children," he gasped. "For their sakes, let me live!"

"I can't," Holmes said stonily.

Accompanied by another outburst of female screams, Holmes picked up Duffee and tossed him overboard.

James McAvoy, whose turn it was next, met his fate with manly calm. "Grant me five minutes to pray," he requested. When he was done, he raised his head and said, "I am ready." Unprotesting, he let Holmes throw him from the boat.

Now Holmes glanced questioningly at Rhodes, who had sat dazed and motionless, watching the terrible drama through dulled eyes. With the first mate incapable of further instructions, Holmes chose the fourth victim himself. He gripped the arm of James Black.

At that, Rhodes roused himself. "No—you must not part man and wife," he commanded.

Holmes released Black. His hand fell upon Frank Askins, who was seated in the middle of the boat. Askins's sisters, Ellen and Mary, defended him frantically, hanging on to Holmes and pleading for mercy. They vowed that if he were hurled overboard, they would join him. Murray tore them loose, and Holmes shoved Askins into the water. Sobbing, the girls jumped after him.

Before the gruesome day was over, Holmes and Murray forcibly drowned eight more men, and the following day four more, all passengers. Every member of the crew had gotten off the *William Brown,* but not a crewman in the longboat was among those cast into the sea.

The sacrifices accomplished their purpose. The lightened longboat rode higher, and chilling swells no longer slopped over the thwarts.

Constant bailing, however, was still necessary to keep ahead of the many leaks.

Holmes was now in complete control. He fashioned a mast out of an oar and hung up a coat for a sail, chiefly as a symbol of hope to his shipmates. The chances of reaching land were a thousand to one.

About midmorning of the third day, Holmes suddenly sprang to his feet. He snatched a shawl from one of the women and waved it wildly above his head. His sharp eyes had spied a ship on the horizon.

She was the *Crescent,* bound from New York to Le Havre, France. The half-frozen occupants of the longboat were taken aboard. Three days later, the jolly boat under Captain Harris was picked up by the *La Mère de Famille* after six days adrift.

Most of those rescued, including Holmes, Rhodes, Murray, and Captain Harris, soon returned to the United States. Word of the tragedy had arrived ahead of them.

The public raised an outcry over the mass drownings. One newspaper called it "wholesale murder of innocent people whom it was the duty of the ship's officers and crew to protect."

Holmes alone was singled out for blame and arrested.

Captain Harris and First Mate Rhodes, who had been responsible for the fatal decision, gave statements to the Attorney General's office. Then they took berths on the *Harry F. Thompson* and sailed off to South America. James Murray, the seaman who had assisted Holmes, disappeared.

After seven months in jail, Holmes was brought to trial on April 13, 1842. By now, the tide of opinion had shifted somewhat in his favor.

Newspapers declared that a "state of nature" had existed in the longboat and pointed out that Holmes had been the only one to act with courage and resolution. He had taken the lives of eighteen persons to save the remaining twenty-five.

But the jury, after twenty-six hours of arguing, found him guilty. The fact that none of the crew had been thrown to the sea counted against him. He was sentenced to six months at hard labor and fined twenty dollars.

Upon his release, he accepted the offer of a berth on a schooner and went back to sea.

The Lone Survivor

As an example of the will to live, Charles F. Tallman has had few equals.

On the day of the great blizzard of January 7, 1866, Tallman was first mate under Captain Leach of the two-masted schooner *Christina*. En route from New York to Boston with a load of cement, the *Christina* had reached Nantucket Sound off the coast of Massachusetts.

Treacherous sandbars dot the area, and the *Christina* was swept onto one—Hawes Shoal. The sides of her hull held against the storm-whipped sea. But within the ship, water rose steadily through the torn bottom.

Tallman knew that if help did not arrive fairly soon, all aboard would drown or freeze to death in the bitter cold. He advised the four other crew members to dress as warmly as possible. Then he began to change into dry clothes.

The men regarded his preparations as useless. In an age when most sailors died at sea, they had the realistic outlook of men to whom daily life is a risk. They recognized the odds against them. They were doomed.

The blizzard closed off sight of land from the ship, and the ship from land. Even if the wreck were seen, the violent seas made rescue impossible. Death was coming whatever they did, the men told Tallman. So let it come quickly.

Tallman nodded his head in understanding, but continued to don layer after layer of clothing. He put on three flannel shirts, two pairs of drawers, a vest, a coat, an overcoat, two pairs of pantaloons, three pairs of socks, heavy boots, and a rubber coat. Having done all there was to do, he got into his bunk.

For the rest of that day, Sunday, the men lay in the upper berths of the ship. With the dawn came a terrifying discovery. The *Christina* had continued to settle during the night. Water was rising swiftly within the cabin.

Forgotten was the brave notion of a quick death. All hands wanted to live! They scrambled onto the deck, through the breakers, and up into the rigging. From high in the shrouds they watched the waves gradually burying the *Christina*.

Captain Leach had lingered below gathering his valuables. When he reached the deck, he had to struggle through shoulder-deep water. Tallman helped him up and tied him fast in the shrouds, just above the clawing wave tips.

"I'm numb all over," the captain mumbled. His clothes were icy hard. The temperature had dropped below freezing.

By now the *Christina* had nearly disappeared. Only the two masts, the jib boom, and the rigging and shrouds rose above the surface. Breakers surged half a mast high.

Tallman stayed with the captain, urging him to shift about as much as he could to keep his blood circulating. But the older man was too weak and gave up the battle. He passed out and died an hour after climbing aloft.

The five crew members left in the rigging clung there desperately, lashed at by wind and snow and salt spray. Late Monday afternoon, two men died. One fell into the water. The other's body hung thirty-five feet above the thundering surf.

Tallman, the cook, and the cabin boy remained. They had gone without sleep, food, or water since Saturday night. Starvation and thirst did not yet threaten them, but sleep meant quick defeat by the conquering cold. They fought to stay awake.

By Tuesday morning they had begun to freeze. That afternoon the cook died, leaving Tallman and the cabin boy. To keep up their spirits, they talked constantly to one another.

The blizzard, if anything, had worsened. The pain of hunger, cold, and cramped muscles was growing unbearable. Tallman and the boy spoke of putting an end to the agony by clasping hands and jumping into the sea.

Suddenly a lull unveiled a bit of land. Tallman had an instant's glimpse of the spires of Osterville, his home town. The sight filled him with longing and revived his will to live. He shouted encouragement to the cabin boy until he realized the lad had stopped answering. He, too, was dead.

High above the sunken ship, with three corpses for companions, Tallman fended off death amid the deafening roar of wind and sea. At daybreak on Wednesday, he could no longer master his thirst. He inched his way down the rigging and broke off chunks of ice frozen to the ratlines just above the water. Greedily he munched and swallowed.

The saltwater in the ice made him violently sick. No sooner had he regained his shaky perch than he began vomiting. But the trip had probably saved his life. It had given him badly needed exercise; the vomiting kept him from getting drowsy.

And he had been seen.

George R. Marchant, lighthouse keeper at Cape Poge, had watched the *Christina* smash into Hawes Shoal. Although an attempt at rescue was out of the question till the weather improved, he had vowed to keep watch through his telescope. Rifts in the storm had allowed him an occasional period of viewing. During one of these, he had followed Tallman's descent to the ratlines.

It seemed unbelievable. The wreck still held life!

Throughout Wednesday, Tallman withstood the storm. He secured his position by forcing his arms through the futtock shrouds and twisting his feet in the rigging below. Thanks to the extra clothes he had put on, his body was warm enough, but his hands and feet were frozen—his feet had got wet, and he had lost his mittens helping Captain Leach. Dangling exhausted and helpless, he wondered if he could last another day.

Thursday morning—his fourth day in the masts—found him partly blinded by the coating of frozen salt spray that covered his face.

The wind had calmed. Through slitted eyes he saw the sun rise, and as the light gathered, something else.

Coming toward him was a whaleboat!

An hour before daybreak, six lifesavers, alerted by the lighthouse keeper, had pushed off from the wharf at Edgartown. Tallman saw them pull alongside. He tried to shout, but could scarcely make a sound. His jaws were frozen together.

A ghastly thought struck him. Would they take him for dead and return to shore?

"I'm alive!" his brain shouted. "Dear God . . ."

All at once a rope was being fastened under his armpits. He heard the cry, "Lower away!"

His head tilted back and he looked skyward and saw the body of the cook jackknifed above him. As he was lowered, he passed the cabin boy. Ten feet more and he passed Captain Leach, hanging by his knees, head down and arms rigidly outstretched toward the deck. The body was naked. The storm and the battering sea had stripped off every shred of clothing.

Tallman was laid in the whaleboat. His face was an icy mask. He could neither talk nor move. Frostbite had swollen and blackened his hands. The tips of several fingers lacked flesh where he had knocked them against the mast to retain circulation.

It was necessary to amputate both his feet and the tips of all ten fingers to save him. He never went back to sea. Crippled, he hobbled on crutches the rest of his life.